Letters to E.T.™

Library of Congress Catalog Card Number 83-42591
ISBN 0-399-12818-2

BOOK DESIGN BY BERNARD SCHLEIFER

Printed in the United States of America

Letters to E.T.™

Letters

to E.T.™

Introduction by
Steven Spielberg

G. P. PUTNAM'S SONS

NEW YORK

Library of Congress Catalog Card Number 83-42591
ISBN 0-399-12818-2

BOOK DESIGN BY BERNARD SCHLEIFER

Printed in the United States of America

To the fans

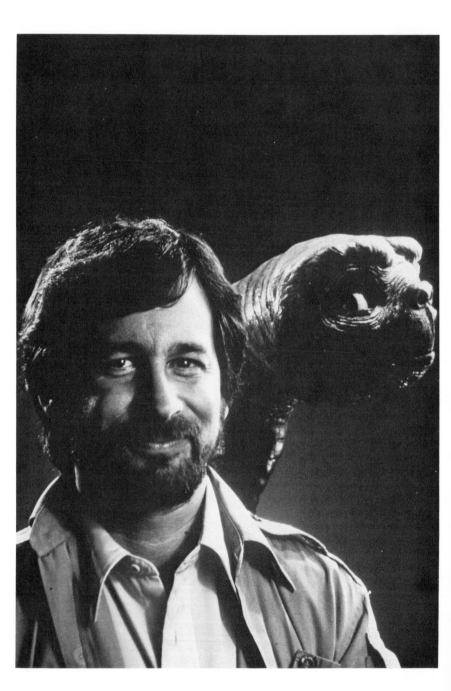

INTRODUCTION
by Steven Spielberg

steven spielberg

March 3, 1983

Dear E.T.,

   I know that you are the shy type, humble even, and that you would blush at any mention of, well, greatness. But, I think you would like to know that you seem to have acquired more than a few earthly fans. They write letters. Tons of them. You get letters from boys, girls, men and women. Letters which are funny, touching, curious, and even weird. I know, I read them when I am missing you. There are letters full of belief, wishes and hope. There are letters full of questions. And, there are questions full of answers.

   So, we've made this book of letters— some of our favorite messages to you. I'm putting this book in an empty bottle, corking it up and flinging it into our ocean of stars.

Maybe one day it will wash up on your far
away shore.

Love,

Steven Spielberg

STEVEN SPIELBERG

P.S. Write when you find work.

Letters to E.T.™

Monday, July 26, 1982

Dear Mr. Spielberg,

I am a little old lady 73½ and I went to see your movie *E.T.* I loved the movie, but when you "pushed my cry button," I lost my two contact lenses that I have to wear after cataract surgery. Since they cost $325 each, I thought just MAYBE you would like to help me pay for two new ones. Oh yes, I also had to pay $1.50 (Senior admission) to see the movie, but since I didn't "see" the whole movie, I'm out that too. It will cost me another $1.50 to see it again. After I lost the lenses, I missed about 20 minutes of the movie.

Sincerely,

Mrs. Vera Binder

September 23, 1982

Dear E.T.

I am writing to tell you in the movie I saw you when you died. I love you we're going to play Pac-Man. I won. I love you so much E.T.. I wish you could come then we could play E.T. cards. And we could see the picture of you. And we could play games too it would be fun. And have a snack too. No beer E.T.. I could dress you up and you could play dolls. Me and you could take a walk too. And we could play house too and it would be fun.

by by by by by by by by by by by by by by by
X O X O X O X O X O X O X O X O X O X O
X O X O X O X O X O X O X O X O X O X O

Love

Melissa

Dear E.T.

Can I call you E.T.? If my name was E.T. I'd let you call me that.

I hope you can read English. That's the only way I know how to write.

If you decide to come back to earth and live here, you might have to get a job. Why don't you be a doctor? I've seen you heal wounds before. Maybe you can find a cure for the common cold. Maybe somebody will explain to you what that is. Maybe you could be a florist. I hear you are an expert at that. Don't let our unemployment rate discourage you.

Have you met Mork from Ork? He flies around in an egg. On earth eggs are sort of egg-shaped.

You ought to go on a national tour of the United States. You could appear in Las Vegas. (Those funny looking robots with one arm are called slot machines. They are used for gambling.)

I bet you made lots of money from your movie. Steven Spielberg can show you how to use it. You can buy yourself a Bell phone so you can phone home when you need to.

You ought to have your own television special. You can have Yoda as your guest.

Well, I have to go now. Write back, okay? I hope you know how to hold a pencil.

So long.

Mitchell

September 28, 1982

Dear E.T.,

I want you to come to Earth so you can go to the school and meet my friends. We will have a lot of fun together. I would go to Mars with you. I will go and get a jacket. When we come from Mars I will go and eat hot dogs and ask you if you want a hot dog.

Your friend,

Tony

October 8, 1982

Mr. Spielberg:

Your movie *E.T. The Extra-Terrestrial* is in a class all by its wonderful self. Through E.T. and Elliott you teach us a very beautiful and valuable lesson: That love is truly universal. Because of the way our world is today, if there would be anything that would prevent us from totally destroying it and each other, it would have to be universal love. Maybe there are beautiful space travelers just like E.T. who will one day come to our world and show us how to really love one another and rid our world of hate once and for all. I really hope so.

Sincerely,

Howard Reabe

P.S. To date, I've seen *E.T.* twenty-two times. I just can't get enough of that beautiful little creature. If you ever make a sequel to *E.T.*, I would give anything to have a part in the movie along with that beautiful little angel of the stars. Please take this into consideration. Thank you.

Sept. 14, 1982

Dear E.T.,

I love your movie and my little brother is crazy about it. His favorite candy is Reese's pieces. Our class has been reading the artical in the news paper about you and love it. Down here you are very famous. About all the walls in our school has something about you or something to do with you. My friends and I want you to make another movie entitled *E.T. part II.* My friends and I hope you take that under consideration. Oh yea tell Elliott and your fan club hello for me O.K.

Sencerly,

Walter

E.T.

FROM DARE

9 YRS. OLD

To E.T.,

I know you are a smart little fellow. You are a great actor. I think your movie was the best I have seen. I thought I saw your space ship one time. I see you in the newspapers. I hope I see you again. GOOD BEYE!

Daren

Dear E.T.

Haven't been to a movie in years much less ever written a fan letter. I was persuaded by a friend to see *E.T.* and became enamoured of your charm, not to mention the magnificent music of John Williams.

Being a recent widow and an alien I understand you completely.

You have become my talisman of hope in an otherwise dreary future.

I am interested in your fan club. If I can do anything to help E.T., call me,

Cynthia Lancaster Norway

I am 64 years young. I saw the movie *E.T.* and enjoyed it so much.

Consider me a fan of *E.T.*

Thank you,

Mrs. Ruth Ambrocelli

Dear E.T.,

I love you and I miss you.

I am collecting cards with your picture on them.

Someday I will come and visit you, and I will bring my little sister Renée and my baby brother Marc. I will bring you a flower too.

LOVE

ELISE

5 yrs old.

9/7/82

Dear Mr. SPIELBERG

I know you must get millions of letters and I really hope you read this one. I am a 13 year old boy who used to be closed off to the world. I didn't care about grades, I just didn't care that much about life. About the only things I did care about was God, Drawing and if my D&D character could get passed 3rd level.

Until one day my Mom took me to see *E.T.* and for the first time I can remember since I broke my arm three years ago I cried and I felt happy. Later on I thought about really becoming successful in Life about the only thing I was good at was Drawing so I thought why can't I be the next Carlo Rambaldi. And after that I changed my grades from D to B+.

Every time after that if I felt bad I would go see *E.T.* again so far I've seen it 4 times and every time I cried.

    I LOVE
    E.T.

      Thank you

      from Kirk

I PRAY that you will *PLEASE* Write back and *PLEASE* SEND Autograph

Kirk

E.T.

THE
EXTRA TERRESTRIAL

THANK
YOU

Berry's World

© 1982 by NEA, Inc.

Dear Mr. Spielberg,

I am only one of the many people who write you to plainly say Thank you. Even though I'm only fourteen I loved your movie *E.T.* It made a part of me I didn't think I had come alive, if that makes any sense. After the first time I saw it, I knew right away it was my favorite movie. You should see my room, I guess you could call me an E.T. fanatic. I've got newspaper clippings of the movie on my wall that I plan to have laminated. Although I don't know what it is, the movie had special meaning to me. All you guys did an excellent job on it, you had laughter and sadness combined in such a way the movie becomes something you'll remember for the rest of your life.

In case you're wondering, I had my mom help me with a little bit of this letter—which hopefully will reach you—

So far I saw *E.T.* 4 times, 3 times with my friend Chris and once with my family, and I loved it each time. The second time I saw it with Chris, even though we were the first ones in line we had to wait more than two hours to see it.

If you do get this letter I would really like it if you could send me a response. I bet everyone that writes you asks you to do that, that's a lot of writing. Oh, I know this is kind of strange to ask but could you maybe send me Henry Thomas's address so I can write him.

I think I speak for everybody when I say once again Thank you.

Rob

P.S. It's supposed to be Robert but all my friends call me Rob. And I'm 14 years old.

To: Steven Spielberg
from: Val

———————→

Dear E.T. Fan Club (and Mr. Spielberg),

I am Tommy's mother. I am writing this letter for him as Tom has never really learned to write much more than his first name. Tom is 20 and autistic. That means he prefers his own strange world to the real one outside himself. Since he has always enjoyed movies filled with special effects, spacecrafts and startling aliens, it was only natural for his parents to take turns waiting in the long lines for *E.T.* In the darkened theater, Tommy came out of himself. He screamed—he clapped—he laughed . . . and then—yes—Tommy cried. Real tears. Autistics do not weep—not for themselves or any others. But Tommy wept and Tommy talked—nonstop—about E.T. . . . Tom has seen *E.T.* three times now and is prone to touching fingers with others and solemnly repeating, "Ouch."

E.T. has changed Tommy's life. It has made him relate to something beyond himself. It's as though Tommy has also been an alien life-form and trying to find his way home—just like E.T.

Totally yours,

Ann Andonian

Dear E.T.,

I love you and I want you to come to my house on Christmas Day and spend the night with me case I get scared. E.T. I love you.

Love,

Heidi

September 14, 1982

Dear E.T.

I think you're cute and funny. Where do you come from? What are your friends like? What is your Space Ship like? How fast can your Space Ship fly? What is your home like? What language do you speak? How do you like earth? Maybe you can't answer all of these questions but just answer some of them, and please send me a small tollken of something.

Sincerely,

Mark

Dear E.T.
My 4 year old
granddaughter and I
have seen your movie
5 times.
She really loves you,
She wrote the note
on the back — by herself.
Please write to
her.
Love
Betty and Holly

THE FAMILY CIRCUS®　　By Bil Keane

9-7

"I heard a strange noise out in the garage."

I am going to put only nine words after this because they say it all. If you people don't bring E.T. back I'll cry.

Sincerely yours,

Teresa

Dear Mr. Spielberg

My name is Daniel I am eight years old. I read about E.T. in *People* magazine. I feel very sad for E.T. all alone in the warehouse. I have just the place for him to come and visit. Between my bed and my dresser is a space just the size for E.T. I have a older brother (17) and two sisters (13) (19) and they will help me make sure that nobody pulls E.T.'s neck out. Also I will have Reese's pieces ready for him. I have seen the movie *E.T.* four times. Please answer before September so that we can have time together. I won't take E.T. to School.

P.S. You can take E.T. back when you need him for his next movie.

P.S. You can trust me.

Daniel

Dear Mr. Spielberg,

I realize this letter must be one of thousands you have received since the release of *E.T.* And it's really not that extraordinarily different from most of those letters. I suppose I could quite truthfully rant and rave about what a marvelous movie *E.T.* is and what exceptional talent you have demonstrated in your direction of it, but I won't.

When I was a child growing up I dreamed of meeting life from other worlds. I can remember staring off into the heavens outside my window and hoping if I wished hard (and sincerely) enough that the inhabitants of the planetary system circling the only star I could see through my elm tree would come and visit me.

I would go out at dusk and string yards of brightly colored wires on my dilapidated wire mesh fence. Maybe by some miraculous freak of physics I could somehow send a message to my star. And They would come.

Now the wires are gone, and the fence shows no signs of the enormous weight of dreams it once bore. The elm tree that once blocked all stars but my own got Dutch elm disease and lets hundreds of stars shine through its branches. And I have grown old, keeping childhood dreams hidden and tucked away.

E.T. found that favorite fantasy and let me live it again. You did justice to the dream of a child.

THANK YOU, STEVEN SPIELBERG.

Rita Calm

Dear E.T.

1 E.T. I hope you are a nice animal
2 I have seen you at the movey
3 are you a very nice creacher
4 E.T. I want you to come over my house
  one day
5 I live on Ruby Street
6 Call me one day my fon namder is
  555-5249
7 E.T. I love you very much
8 I hope I see you one day

Deanna Marie

7 yrs. old

Dear E.T.,

I hope there is going to be a *E.T.*, 2. I loved the movie *E.T.*, it was exciting. I liked when you were riding on the bike, and thanks for not dying.

Your friend,

Jonah

P.S. Next time your in the neiborhood, E.T., phone me.

Jonah

Age 8

To E.T.

Hi!

How are you? Did you have a safe trip home? July 21 which is my brithday I seen your movie.

I have twelve packs of your cards which is a hundred cards. When is your brithday?

Will you send me your autogragh and Mr. Spielberg's autogragh.

Mr. Spielberg your movie *Raiders of the Lost Ark* should have won best movie of the year.

please write back
and please send me
your autograghs

your friend Michael

Dear E.T.

I am 10 years old and in the 5th grade, I saw *E.T.* 2 times and my cousin Jenny looks just like Gertie.

This summer I went camping and I put a bag of Reese's pieces on the table and in the morning they were gone! Did you eat them?

You are the best creature on earth (or in space) *E.T.* is better than all the movies ever made put together.

I would love to see you real.

Your friend forever,

Peter

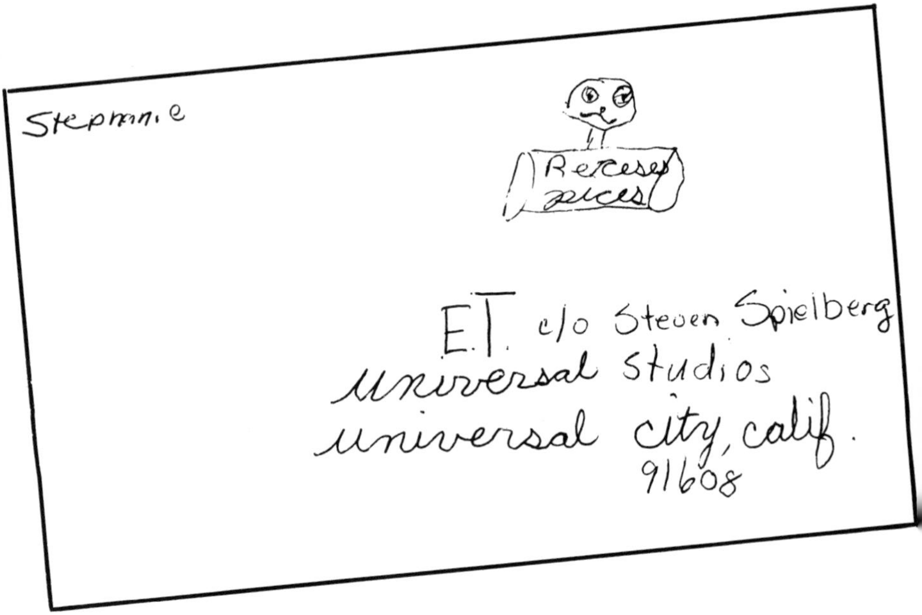
Stephanie
E.T. c/o Steven Spielberg
universal Studios
universal city, calif.
91608

Dear E.T.

Your invited to my birthday party and we will have Reese's pieces and pizza and Beer. I love you. Your so cute.

on March 27, 1983
at 1:00 to 5:00

please come

from:

Stephanie

Dear E.T.
I have Braces.
I Got them yesterday.
I am home from
School because my
mouth. is sore.
I am seven years
old.
do you have teeth?

From John

STEVEN SPIELBERG
E.T. 1982

Doug Short

VIDEO | CABLE | MUSIC | TALENT | STAGE

VARIETY

PRICE
$1.25
NEWS~~~~~~
Second Cla~~

Published Weekly at 154 West 46th Street, New York, N.Y. 10036 by Variety, Inc. Annual subscription, $40. Single copies $1.25.
Second Class Postage Paid at New York, N.Y. and at additional Mailing Offices
©COPYRIGHT, 1982, BY VARIETY, INC.; ALL RIGHTS RESERVED

New York, Wednesday, July 7, 1982

USPS 454-960

THE SPACEMAN THAT SAVED H'WOOD

~~~~~ SUCCESS SPOIL THE ET?!

**Grownup Pix
Sick; Kid
Stuff Socko**

Dear E.T.

   You were a great preformer in *E.T.*, *Empire Strikes Back* and *Star Wars*. I bet you hav more talent than alot of people. I am incoraged to go see you preform in any movie.

Love,

Michelle

Please write back!!!!

Dear E.T. Fan Club,

I only saw *E.T.* once and I loved it. I would like to know more about your fan club. Can you please send more information about it? Could you please give my picture to E.T. or Steven Spielberg.

I think. . . . .

E.T. is

I've got a two year old cousin who runs around saying E.T., E.T.! He also calls fire plugs E.T.

E.T.'s biggest fan,

Jeff

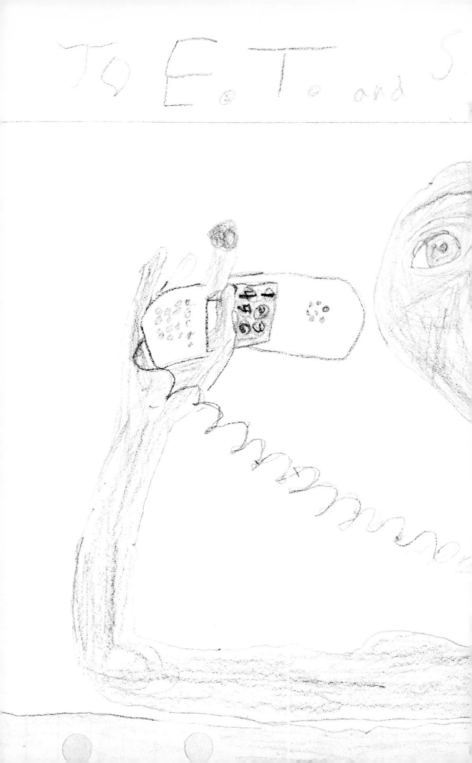

even Spielberg

m Jeff

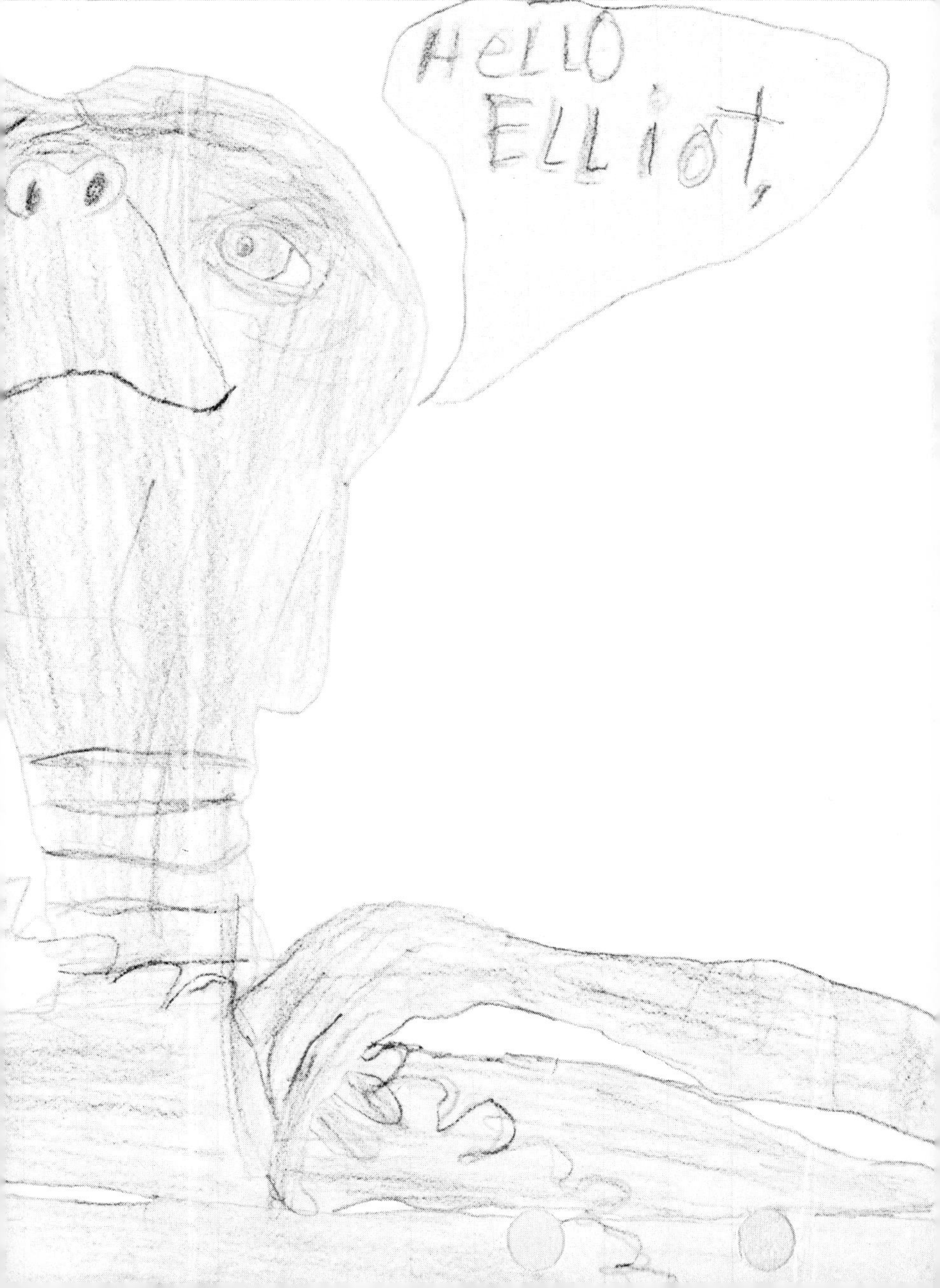

Sept. 14, 1982

Dear E.T.

I want to be in a movie with you. You are beutiful. To me E.T. means love. Where do you come from? I would love to have a picture of you and Elliott if it is possible. My name is Katherine. I am 9 years old. I would like your autagragh. Where can I write to join the E.T. fan club? I would like to know more about you. You are a great actor/actress. Can you skate? If you can come to my skating party in November on the 16th please come.

Love

Katherine

THE FAMILY CIRCUS®   By Bil Keane

"And I wasn't even allowed to keep a FROG in my room!"

E.T.
THE EXTRA-TERRESTRIAL
Storybook

Featuring photographs from Steven Spielberg's magical film.

Sept. 8, 1982

Dear E.T.

I liked your movie very much. I liked the way you talk. E.T. what do you like to do with your powers. E.T. is success important to you. I got a shirt like you. My name is Cindy I am in 3rd Grade. I want to be famous like you. You are better than Annie. I got a book about you. good-by

your friend Cindy

Cindy

P.S. I am reading a book about you.

Dear E.T.

I love you forever E.T. I wish you come back from the space ship

Love

Kendra
5 yrs old

P.S. Can I have a E.T. doll

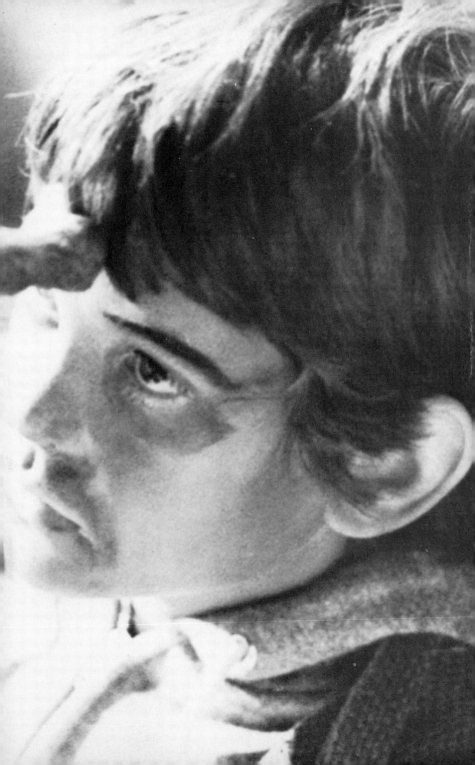

Hi! E.T.

I am Justin. I am 4 years old. I saw you at the show. I love you. Come and visit me during the day not at night. Also E.T. come without your costume and bring it so I can try it on for Halloween.

I love you,

Justin